Remarkable Moments from 30,000 Hours in the Cockpit

LADDIES
IN WAITING

TOMMY TINKER
Kohala Hale Publications / Kapaáu, Hawaii

Copyright © 2018 by **Tommy Tinker**

All rights reserved. No part of this publication may be reproduced, distributed or transmitted in any form or by any means, without prior written permission.

Kohala Hale Publications
P.O. Box 599
Kapaáu, HI 96755

Acknowledgements
On the Cover: I chose this great shot of Col. John "Jake" Kapowich, one of my COs from VMA 133 - standing with a Douglas A-4 Skyhawk - because the plane, the flight suit and the swagger epitomize the squadron that flew out of Oakland and Alameda, California. Plus, Jake was much better looking than I.

Publisher: Rebecca Tinker Coburn
Graphic Designer: Trish Heaney
Back cover photo: Bridget Oates

Laddies in Waiting / Tommy Tinker -- 1st edition
ISBN 978-0-692-16909-4

PREFACE

The original stories were sent to friends and family, as they were completed, in a series of emails over many months called "Monday Mail." The book title, *Laddies in Waiting,* refers to VMF 133, the reserve Marine Attack Squadron I was attached to for fifteen years, waiting to be called up to go to war. We never were, thank God!

"Where do we get such men?"
James Michener, *The Bridges at Toko-Ri*

"Well, to start, you put them in a plane that breaks on take off!"
Tommy Tinker, in answer to the question

CONTENTS

Second Lt. Tinker, USMC	1
Travels with Charlie	5
Marine Corps Air Station Kaneohe Bay	9
Molokai Express	14
Iwakuni, Japan	18
Gear Up Landing	23
Maui Divers	27
VMA 133: Ken D	30
VMA 133: Phil Delano	35
VMA 133: John B.	38
VMA 133: 6G-28, or Broke on Takeoff	43
VMA 133: Tony, MCAS El Toro	47
Funny, Dumb Stunts	65
Life After Death	69
Challenger Disaster	71
SMX Crash	73
Medford to Crescent City, 1960: Advances in Technology	75
Chico to Marysville, 1960	79
Night Flight	82
Pilot Pushing	84
Blossom Flights	87
Formation Approach to SFO	89
You *Can* Teach an Old Dog New Tricks	91
Interesting Day at the Office (Honolulu to Sydney)	94

LADDIES
IN WAITING

1
SECOND LT. TINKER, USMC

After graduating from Edna High School in 1951, I tried to get my father to let me attend the E. R. Cross School of Diving in Los Angeles. My dad said no, that I needed to get a college degree first, and after that he didn't care what I did. So, I entered Victoria Jr. College, in Victoria, TX, and at the end of my second year I got a draft notice, which changed my life's track! I earned a high grade on the written test and the recruiter talked me into going to the Navy flight school in Pensacola, FL.

Flight school was a blast and very exciting. OMG! The very first person I got into a military aircraft with was Major John Glenn! Unfortunately, we only had a one-sided conversation. I sat in the front seat, got air sick, and listened as John (he said I could call him John - ha ha!) flew us around and pointed out the different areas and airfields I would be working with.

I think my flight school experience was fairly average, although in basic training one of my friends had to bail out of a plane that was in an "inverted" flat spin and died when his chute failed to open. Additionally, I almost killed myself in advanced training on my first jet formation takeoff.

One of the pre-takeoff procedures in the T-33 was to turn off the hydraulic power to the ailerons, then move the controls to make sure we still had at least minimal movement. My incident happened because I forgot to turn the hydraulic power back on after the check! Fortunately, during the takeoff, I was on the right side of the flight instructor's plane and the other cadet was on his left. I say fortunately because, due to a fueling error, I had more fuel (weight) in the right wing tip tank than the left, and as we lifted off the runway, my plane went into about a 45 degree right bank and turn, which I couldn't control because the ailerons had no hydraulic power. I remember the instructor looking straight down at me with his mouth open! If I had been on the left side, there could have been at least one, if not two, mid-air collisions as I flew through the other two planes, leaving three pilots dead. I would have made history!

Headline: Tinker Causes Worst Crash in Naval Aviation History!

Didn't happen, thank God. Hell, I didn't even kill myself. I kicked in full left rudder and all the left aileron available. Pilots on the runway behind me said my right wing tip was only a foot off the ground. As the airspeed increased, aileron control also increased, so the plane gradually became wings-level. Now I was able to get a free hand to turn the hydraulic power lever back on and rejoin my flight. It was the only "below average" score I got in flight school, and I was glad to be around to get it!

Carrier Landings

In the mid 1950s, when I went through flight school, it was still required that all Naval aviators, including those of us that had decided to accept a commission in the Marine Corps, got at least six landings on an aircraft carrier. (Did you know that Marines are actually part of the Navy?) With only about 150 hours in my log book, five other cadets and I walked on board the aircraft carrier USS Monterey to acquire our requisite landings. It wasn't going to be easy!

The way it worked was that six of us would go to sea on the ship then six other cadets would fly out and make their landings. Then my group would man those airplanes, make our six landings and fly back to Pensacola. It didn't work that smoothly though. After my group of six had our pre-flight briefing, we all went topside to watch the six cadets coming from shore make their landings. It was a pretty interesting show as the first plane trying to land was waved off by the LSO (Landing Signal Officer), and the second plane spun in and crashed in the ocean. He evidently survived, but we were all pretty much in shock. Holy shit! Looked like we were going to be one airplane short.

2
TRAVELS WITH CHARLIE

In mid-June 1955, the same day that my mother pinned Navy Wings of Gold on my fresh, USMC Second Lt. body, I bought an airplane. It was a $600, 600-pound, 65-horsepower, two-place, fabric and wire, 1946 built, tail-dragging Taylorcraft I called Charlie. This little plane cruised at 95 mph, which was quite good considering the most popular light plane of the day, the Piper Cub, was at least 20 mph slower. The young man I bought it from took me around the pattern for one landing, then got out and handed me the keys. This was going to be quite a transition since the last aircraft I flew was a single engine jet that had a landing speed of 110 knots and tricycle landing gear.

(Over the years, I have owned five light planes. Not one of them had lights or a radio, and most were in the $600 to $800 range. Each one has a story worth its own chapter. Two of them were involved in non-injury crashes - someone else was flying them - but were repaired and flown again.)

With a 30-day leave before reporting to my next duty station, my intent was to spend time with my folks while trying to impress the girls with my new status and not kill myself in my new airplane (which was a distinct possibility). But now, flying from Corpus Christi and looking down at brown water through a mostly undercast cloud deck, I started to be concerned about my next landing. I had made arrangements with a fellow to use his pasture for my airport; it was a grass field that would give me about 1600 ft. to operate out of. The T-craft stalled (viciously) at 40 mph, but would float forever at 55. It took me three passes before I finally got slow enough that when I pulled the power the plane would land.

The days went by fast and the flying was fun! I landed on the beaches on the barrier islands around Aransas Pass and Corpus Christi, buzzed some old girlfriends' houses (hope their husbands didn't mind), got several of my friends to throw up, and all in all made a pest of myself. Then suddenly it was time for Charlie and me to head west to California.

Since the fuel consumption of the Continental engine was slightly over 4 gph, and we only carried about 12 gallons, we would be making a lot of stops, flying about 250 miles per leg. We mostly stopped for fuel, but as I approached Uvalde, TX, the terrain started to look funny, like it was bubbling! I had never seen mountains before. I landed just to get my nerve up.

I was using an old map and some of the planned fueling stops no longer had fuel or were even still airfields! At one place, I was in a bind because I needed gas and couldn't find the airport that was shown on the map. As I circled, I finally saw an old wind sock without the fabric - just the wire ribs were left. I could also see tracks where planes used to land. I did. Then I hitchhiked into town and came back with five gallons of regular gas, so was able to proceed on westward.

The first night was spent in El Paso, where I flew around until the tower gave me a green light to land. The next day, I went into ops to check on the weather and saw a group of military enlisted guys looking for a ride out west. I chose the Marine because we were going to the same place. He was an okay companion, but there was one glitch. He had some flying time under his belt - not much, and only in an Erocoupe. *(Most have probably never heard of it, but it was a cute little two-place side-by-side with twin vertical tails. The unique thing about this plane was that the ailerons and rudder had an interconnect, so you only had to steer it like a car and the correct amount of rudder would automatically be added for the amount of aileron you used.)*

Well, human nature is really interesting because as soon

as we left the ground from the El Paso Airport, this Private and my Second Lt. self became *equals* in the realm of flying, and had several small disagreements over decision making. About an hour from Tucson International Airport, we came upon a range of mountains that should not have been an issue, but a cloud cover above us forced us into flying down a canyon, searching for a way through. It rapidly got so narrow that I became concerned about our ability to turn around and head back out. My "equal" wanted to continue through a small hole in the ridge, and at that point I pulled rank, made the turn to fly north and go around that whole mountain range, then head west again. Even with the extra distance, we did make it to Tucson with an unknown amount of fuel remaining.

Next, we fueled at Yuma, AZ, El Centro, CA, and then ended the adventure at our destination, Orange County Airport, CA. Within a month, I was based in Hawaii and had to sell Charlie at a huge loss! (Not really.)

3
MARINE CORPS AIR STATION KANEOHE BAY

I was so lucky! One of my biggest concerns about choosing the Marine Corps instead of the Navy was that I would be based on the East Coast, and I really wanted to stay out west. Boy, did I get west... all the way out to Hawaii.

Once there, I was assigned to the VMF 232, at MCAS Kaneohe on Oahu, which was flying the Marine Corps version of the F-86, called the FJ-2. This was not a new airplane (it fought the MiG 15 in Korea) but it was famous for being the first aircraft to go through the speed of sound. Yes, even before Yeager in the X-15! It was designed with a unique flying tail that could reach out of the shock wave produced approaching Mach 1, and continue to control the aircraft. The FJ-2 made aviation history.

And it got me through the speed of sound.

I went past Mach 1 three times. You climb to 40,000', nose over to about 30 degrees down, full power and watch the airspeed move up. About Mach .94 the rudder would vibrate. About .97 you lost control of your ailerons. So, when you did it with a flight of four aircraft, you needed to spread out because some airplanes went left and some went right. Once you got up to Mach 1, all this ceased and the airplane started to "fly right" again. As you continued the dive to lower altitudes, the friction of the thicker atmosphere would slow the craft back below Mach 1, and the plane would wander and vibrate again as you reduced your Mach number accordingly. It was an honor to get to do it in the model aircraft that accomplished it first!

The other great attraction that Hawaii had was SCUBA diving (Self Contained Underwater Breathing Apparatus.) In 1955, we formed a club called the "AKU Marines". (AKU is a Hawaiian fish.) At that time, were on the "cutting edge" of the science, much like Yeager was in flying, because Cousteau & Gagnan developed the Aqua-lung regulator, which allowed man to explore another part of our world we were restricted from!

We lost a few guys during the two years I was in VMF 232; one just didn't come back after launching on a solo night flight. After days of searching, we found no trace, just silence. Another friend was flying the piston powered AD-1 when the engine blew up! With fire in his face, the water landing/ crash was fatal. A third was killed on an instrument approach at night when he lost visual reference to level flight (cockpit lights were out). And a fourth was killed by a wake turbulence upset during a formation takeoff.

There were several non-fatal crashes too. One pilot got below the power/drag curve and left his landing gear and external wing fuel tanks in Kaneohe Bay, while the rest of the aircraft made it onto the runway!

Kaneohe 1956 – Richard

"Whiskey Tango 14 ready for takeoff." "Roger Whiskey Tango 14. Cleared for takeoff runway 4." When in position, the section leader signals to Richard, his wingman, to come up on the engine power. They then check each other's aircraft for obvious problems, like flap settings, fuel leaks, open panels, etc. After exchanging thumbs up, they release the brakes and start the takeoff roll. Approaching 120 knots (and the end of the runway), they rotate nose up to a flight attitude, and that is when Richard realizes that his ailerons are jammed and won't move! He has no choice but to abort the takeoff. Without enough room remaining to stop, he ends up sliding off the runway into the Pacific Ocean!

This is the way the accident was described by one of our pilots who saw it: "It was a movie crash! I walked down to look at it - wings sheared off between two rocks, then the front of the plane up to the cockpit crushed by other rocks, and finally, what was left (just a bent up fuselage and a beat up pilot) went into the ocean." When the waves came in they would cover the cockpit and Richard. When they retreated he could breath. I think his oxygen mask also helped. Luckily, a fisherman who was on the beach at the crash site expedited Richard's recovery and probably saved his life!

I am not sure what the full extent of Richard's injuries was. I do remember visiting him in the hospital and know that he had a detached retina in at least one of his eyes because of the rapid deceleration. (Can you imagine going from a speed of 120 MPH to 0 in the width your house?) I think he made a full recovery, but I left for duty in Japan soon after, so don't know if he was able to return to the VMF 232 squadron family.

Kaneohe 1957 - Rick Vaum

Another section (two-aircraft) takeoff. This time, the aircraft are the FJ-4, a newer and more powerful model of the FJ-2. As the two aircraft accelerate to takeoff speed, Rick stays close to the skipper's wing. As they rotate to lift off, the wake turbulence from the lead aircraft flips Rick's aircraft upside down on the runway, killing him instantly.

Kaneohe 1957 - Art Ford

On a night section approach to Kaneohe MCAS, the wingman, Art Ford, was having problems with his instrument panel lighting. The white lights that could be dimmed were not working, and the only others available were bright red flood lights that blinded him to outside references. So, since he was flying on the section leader's wing, the logical solution was to just turn off all cockpit lighting and use the skipper's aircraft for his attitude reference. Unfortunately, during the approach, the flight went into a heavy rainstorm and Art lost sight of the lead aircraft. What the radar monitors saw was a secondary target (Art) moving to the right away from the primary target. Very shortly thereafter, the secondary target disappeared! No wreckage was ever found.

4
MOLOKAI EXPRESS

The second light aircraft I owned was in Hawaii in 1956. Four of us from the squadron went together to buy a 1941 built, three-place Piper J-5 (later designated PA-12). It wasn't in flyable condition though because the fabric covering the wings needed to be removed and replaced, which is fairly complicated. Fortunately, we found a sergeant in our squadron who knew how to do it, so with his direction and help we soon had a beautiful little ship. We painted the new wing covering with a big orange and white sunburst design, the idea being that if we went down in the ocean we might have better luck at being spotted!

    I can't remember all the co-owners but Tom Johnson

was one, and I think there was a ground officer, and maybe Ken Scarborough. The reason I think of Ken is I remember he and I taking the plane up to Kahuku Point, which used to be an airport, but when we landed there a radio transmission tower had been set up, so we had to avoid a lot of cables on takeoff and landing. Ken and I shut the plane down and went to see the huge waves rolling in at the point. When we got back to the Piper, there were two cows trying to chew the ailerons off the wings. Fortunately, we hadn't stayed and watched the ocean too long!

All you ex-military folks might remember Major/Colonel/General (I think) O'Donnell. He was one of the lucky few that got to ride in the Piper: the story is that a twin Beech crashed at night flying an instrument approach at (again) Kahuku Point with about five fatalities. Major O'Donnell was leading the investigation board and he asked if I would fly him over the crash site. I actually got to fly the approach profile in my J-5 and the major had a broad grin on his face the whole time. I still don't know how he got his big self in my aircraft!

Molokai Express

The Kaneohe civilian airport is a 1600-foot dirt strip with electric power lines at the far end. Winds are calm when we start our takeoff roll. The three Hawaiian spear guns with their 7-foot long shafts are stowed along the whole length of the cabin, including under the rudder pedals. Three scuba tanks and my two dive buddies are secured behind me, which probably moves our center of gravity dangerously aft, and I don't have time to ask where the rest of our gear is because I am committing to go.

The tail finally comes up and I drag the Piper in the air with no room to spare. Turning in a shallow left bank allows us to fly over fences and under power lines as we head for the "Friendly Island" of Molokai. At 700 feet, we find ourselves in an inversion - an area of warmer air - and the engine starts to overheat, which stops our climb. We struggle with this for about ten minutes and finally work our way higher into cooler air to cruise at 2000 feet, which is the traffic pattern altitude for Molokai Municipal Airport. We spend the night at the Pau Hana Inn (the name means "through with work") and the next morning fly down to the airport that serves the leper colony at Kalaupapa.

You can't be a beginner if you dive Kalaupapa! I have a DVD made from an old 8mm film that shows us leaping off a cliff with a vertical wall that drops about ten feet into the sea. There were about eight to ten-foot waves pounding the shore – it's always this way. Getting in the water is obviously not a problem but how do we get out? Watching the film, I was reminded how we actually did it 60 years ago. First of all, the sea cliff has to be absolutely vertical. If so, the wave face will not push you into the cliff. It will only pick you up so you can find an opening, which allows you to take off one of your flippers. Then, when the wave picks you up again, you can stick your foot in the opening you've selected and hold onto the top of the wall. When the wave drops away again, you just roll yourself up and out of the water. Sure, there are important considerations - most imperatively, that the wall be absolutely vertical! My friend and fellow VMA 232 pilot, Art Ford, was a new diver. Before his plane was lost in 1957, we went diving off MCAS Kaneohe. Heading back in, Art panicked and swam hard for land, climbing out onto a slanted shore. The poor guy ended up with about 50 stitches!

5
IWAKUNI, JAPAN

In early 1957, I transferred from Hawaii to Iwakuni, Japan for my last year of active duty, and became a member of a unit that coordinated control of aircraft during combat situations. We spent a lot of time on ships going from Japan to Okinawa and the Philippines to participate in practice war games. I also spent a bit of time underwater.

Inland Sea, Iwakuni 1957 - M.O. Doyle

The water temperature was about 65 degrees and visibility was maybe 15 feet. Fish life was nil and there were no coral reefs - not much attraction for recreational diving. Unfortunately, diving for fun wasn't the reason we were in the water. Two nights prior, a single-pilot aircraft flying a practice instrument approach had crashed into the Inland Sea, off of Iwakuni. A search party had found an oil slick about three miles off shore, at 60' depth. There were not many divers around, so, since I had started the AKU Marines, a dive club on the base, it was understandable that I was asked to help in the recovery. The other diver was a younger guy that had gone through some formal Navy dive training.

When descending hand over hand down the anchor line in low visibility, the scenario changed every few feet. At about 45', parts of an aircraft start to take shape. The tail section! Lower, the engine. The 18-cylinder Wright engine is lying separated, but close to what is looking like the front of the aircraft. With the poor visibility, it's very confusing. Now, 60 feet down, I can see the wing lying across the fuselage with the landing gear sticking up. (Gear was down, but it is up.) Where is the cockpit? Wait, I'm underneath the upside down wing, so the cockpit must be right HERE!

Poor visibility is the shits. I'm right on top of the poor guy and don't know it. Everything is upside down... trying to figure it out. The body is towards the instrument panel. I read his name on the back of his helmet: *M.O. Doyle.* It's going to be hard to get him out when he is upside down and wants to float. I take the knife off his left shoulder harness and start sawing away at his seat belt (I can reach the belt release, but I don't want to.) Finally, get that cut through and tug on the body, but his legs are still caught. The other diver and I go to the surface and agree on a plan with the guys on the boat, who are all M.O.'s friends and squadron mates.

We'll tie a line to the body so the guys on the boat can pull him out, and also attach a float so if he gets loose he will come to the surface. The only thing is that the boat has to back up current slightly so the pull will be in the right direction and effective. The other diver will have a signal line to the surface: one tug is to start pulling; two tugs are to stop. Down we go. All is set. The line to the body is angled up current, so it looks like the pull will get him free. My dive buddy tugs once, the line tightens and the dead pilot starts out of the aircraft. Only problem is that the surface boat, not having any visual references has now drifted down with the current and M.O.'s body has been partially pulled out, but now, with the changing angle of pull, is pinned against the fuselage and looks like he is going to lose his head!

I look at the other diver who has the signal line and see he's dropped it; I almost rupture a lung getting to the surface to stop the pull. Okay, got to do it myself. Down we go. I tie a line to the body and stand on the wing, brace myself against the right extended landing gear and start to pull. *Hey, it's working! He's coming out!* Not! The whole wing rolls over and I land on my head on the bottom.

About this time, I get low on air. Since the other diver has two tanks, he is still okay. Plus - and I was envious of this - he has a full-face mask. I've always wanted one of those. The inflowing air keeps the mask clear of fog, your jaws don't get tired of clamping down on the mouthpiece, and when diving in polluted water (our current situation), your health is more secure. I signal that I am going after another tank and that I will be right back. On the boat the crew is rigging me another tank when I notice that the line we have hooked to the body is getting slack. Plus, large bubbles of air are breaking the surface. (You could smell decay.) The body pops to the surface followed by our other diver. I look in horror: the full-face mask that I had envied was filled to the eyes with red liquid. *My god! He's ruptured a lung!*

Turns out it wasn't blood, but puke. This poor kid was near the bottom waiting for me, when he felt something bump into his back; turning around, much to his horror, was the object of our dive, with his arms wrapped around him! I am amazed that he didn't drown or suffer an embolism. I am sure he lost control of some of his bodily functions. It was very sad watching the expressions on the faces of M.O.'s friends as they worked to bring their mate's broken body on board.

The last thing I had to do was to return to the submerged aircraft and make observations for the accident report. The procedure, when flying a practice instrument approach, was to wear a hood so he couldn't cheat and look at the horizon. In this case, it was a black piece of cloth folded in half and sewn together in back. When snapped to the glare shield in front and slipped over the helmet, the pilot could keep tension on the hood by holding his head back. This makes it very easy to get rid of the hood if needed (like with vertigo). In this case though, the system worked against him. What I think happened, although I don't know what the accident board decided, was M.O. Doyle was doing a procedure turn outbound, when he got vertigo. The chase pilot said the plane went from a left turn all the way over to the right, then upside down. M.O. threw the hood off and was looking at an overcast night sky. (The hood had dropped over the instrument panel, where I found it between his head and the panel.) There weren't any lights on the surface, so even though he had taken the hood off, he still had no reference to the horizon. Plus the hood was now hanging down over his flight instruments and he had no chance of recovery.

The next time I saw that cockpit was when I was climbing into a similar model airplane in preparation for a night flight. I hadn't thought a thing about it until I swung my right foot over the rail and looked in. I almost canceled the flight!

6
GEAR UP LANDING

I have been cleared for takeoff on Iwakuni's runway 2, holding the brakes and moving the throttle forward to 30 inches of manifold pressure, releasing the breaks and holding full right rudder to counter the torque of the powerful Wright 3350 engine. We start our take off roll. I add power just at the rate the increasing airspeed will allow the full right rudder to keep the plane on the runway. Now, with the engine at full power of 58 inches, the piston-powered AD-6 Skyraider accelerates rapidly and is soon airborne. I start a right turn to leave the traffic pattern and throttle back to climb power setting.

I have nothing to do now except sightsee over the Inland Sea of Japan, as the main purpose of the flight is to stay airborne for at least two hours so I can get my $100 flight pay for the month. That flight pay is actually called "hazardous" pay, and is the main difference between us flyboys and the "grunt" officers. I personally would consider a foxhole hazardous, but what do I know?

Still in my climb and heading north toward Hiroshima, I start a right turn, as we are not supposed to fly over that city. It is 1957 and they are still a little bit sensitive. I'm starting to feel a vibration from the engine and, glancing at my instruments, I notice that the cylinder head temperature is approaching the maximum of 232 degrees. The vibration is from detonation - the cylinders are so hot, the fuel in them is exploding at the wrong time. As I reduce power and start into a descent, I see that the cowl flaps on the engine are open (the right position for engine cooling, so I don't know why it got so hot). But now, in the power-off glide, it is starting to cool down to normal readings.

Heading back to the field, I call the tower and declare an emergency. I notice that there is a multi-engine Navy patrol plane, called a P2-V, in position on the runway where I intend to land. Since I am just descending through 2,000 ft., I won't be there for a couple of minutes so it shouldn't be a problem. As I get to short final at 500 ft., the patrol plane is still sitting there and the tower tells him to clear the runway. The smartass comes back with, "If we clear the runway, there will be two emergencies instead of one."

Since my engine had cooled down, I told the tower that I would try to make a 360° turn to make time for the runway to clear. "Power-up, gear-up," is an automatic reflex we were all taught! I roll into the right turn. When I have turned about 30 degrees, I notice the P2-V had started its takeoff roll, so I reverse my right turn and head back to the runway. As I crossed the landing threshold, the runway duty-watch fires his flare gun and the tower radioed for me to "wave off" (add power and cancel the landing.) My thinking (if you could call it that) was that they both thought I was too close to the P2-V. I was right behind him and fighting his prop wash, but as I slowed and he accelerated, I could see it would work out. Nonetheless, since my engine was down to normal temperature, I added power to go around, but decided to at least get in a touch and go. (I didn't.) So, releasing a little bit of back pressure, I hit the runway with a jolt. My immediate thought was that I needed to have the landing gear oleos pressurized. Then I reached for the gear handle and saw it was already in the up position! I was immediately sopping wet with perspiration!

Since that lovely engine seemed to be purring away with no extra vibration, I decided I might be able to get it back, with the gear down this time. After I passed the departure end of the runway, I made a 90-degree right turn, then a 270-degree left turn, and landed on runway 20. On taxi in, the tower asked me if I had hit the runway.

"Did you see sparks?" I asked.

"Yes!" they replied.

"Yes sir! I hit the runway." I had ground four inches off each of the four prop tips! The Navy pilot got 100% blame for that incident, which I thought was justice.

7
MAUI DIVERS

In August of 1959, the same month I would be hired at Pacific Airlines as a pilot, I made a last ditch effort to salvage my adolescent attempt to make a living in the ocean as a diver. I flew to Maui to talk with Larry Windley, president of Maui Divers, about running their diving operation. I originally met Larry when we were Marines stationed at MCAS Kaneohe on Oahu, and were both members of the SCUBA diving club, AKU Marines, on the base.

My visit turned into just that - a visit - as it was obvious that this black coral harvesting dive operation couldn't continue as it was, having left two out of three divers paralyzed as a result of the bends. And in 1959, alternative harvesting methods (submersibles, robots, etc.) had not been invented. After a "thanks, but no thanks" and a quick visit with Larry, I had the good sense to leave and choose a career in a profession that was a little more conventional.

When Larry and his partner, Jack Ackerman, formed Maui Divers, they did everything water and dive related that would make money, including filming for a couple of movies. Mostly though, diving for black coral, which was made into jewelry and sold from their shop in Lahaina, Maui, provided the majority of the income. The biggest problem with black coral was that harvesting it required diving far below normal "recreational" depths. The divers were descending over 200 feet, at least twice a day, with SCUBA tanks that didn't contain near enough air to allow them to conform to the proper decompression times.

The predictable result was that both Larry and Jack ended up crippled. Larry was on his second dive to 200 feet on the day of his accident. The SCUBA tank, which was only attached to his backpack with a rope, came loose, allowing it to float, and jerking his regulator out of his mouth as it headed for the surface! He chased and caught it at about 80 feet, then continued up to the boat where his crew dragged him onboard. He immediately went into convulsions and ended up in a decompression chamber for over 24 hours. He ended up paralyzed below the waist.

Larry was down but not out. An amazing, interesting

guy, he is acknowledged as a source of information in Gavan Daws' book, *Shoal of Time: A History of the Hawaiian Islands*. Larry also did most of the research to allow Lahaina Town on Maui to be set aside as a historical site. Even being disabled, he continued to forge on until 1964, when he was on a sailboat that was lost in a storm and never seen again! A fitting end for a guy that really pushed the envelope.

8
VMA 133: KEN D

I first met Ken in the summer of 1959, when we both joined Marine Attack Squadron (VMA) 133, a Marine Reserve Squadron flying F2-H Banshees out of the Oakland commercial airfield. During the next eight years or so, we often flew together in two and four-plane formations, and I gradually became aware that when Ken was leading the flight, he sometimes put himself and his wingmen in jeopardy. Some of it was thoughtless chance-taking, like leading a four-plane division of Banshees into mountain canyons at 250 knots (slow), just sightseeing. These aircraft had an ejection seat that needed at least 2,000 feet to have even a small chance of success, and the very real possibility of a bird strike, which could have been fatal, made this a tremendous and needless gamble.

In the early '60s, the squadron moved to Naval Air Station (NAS) Alameda and transitioned to a new aircraft, the Douglas built A4 Skyhawk, a very capable ground support aircraft, which was a lot of fun to fly! At about the same time, the Marine Reserves started to use the Naval air station at Fallon, Nevada for our summer two-week active duty training. My increasing awareness of Ken's "borderline" flight capabilities were enhanced when I flew as his wingman during a botched instrument approach, when he misread the approach diagram and descended below the minimum crossing altitudes (in the mountains) and wasn't aware of it! Fortunately, I had just been given the job of "Safety Officer" for the squadron, and now, not only had an opening, but a duty to talk to Ken about my concerns. I told him of my observations over the last couple of years and pointed out that he demonstrated an overconfidence that was not warranted. He assured me that he was well aware of his shortcomings. So we left it at that.

On Saturday, August 31, 1968, VMA 133 pilots were at NAS Alameda preparing to "evacuate" for our annual active duty to NAS Fallon, Nevada that morning - all of us except for Ken D., who has volunteered to be the Duty Officer that day. He intends to come join the rest of us on Sunday, because he was having some friends over for dinner that evening, and volunteering to stay as Duty Officer, then fly up to Fallon on

Sunday, makes his schedule work.

Ken had just gotten married. His first! His lady is very pretty, vulnerable, and comes with a newborn child, but it's not Ken's. The guy has done a really neat thing by making them family! I am sure he loved them. His dinner guest was interesting; one of the things the two guys had in common was airplanes. As they visited that night, his friend told Ken he had a multi-engine float plane with a mechanical problem, floating on the reservoir in the western Sierra foothills, Hetch Hetchy (the primary water source for San Francisco), and he planned to be up there on Sunday to bring his plane home. As they chatted, Ken told his friend that, on his way to join us at Fallon, he would fly by with his A4 and say hello!

Sunday September 1, Ken left Alameda en-route to join VMA 133 in Fallon. He had two hours of fuel, and the flight would only take forty-five minutes, so he had lots of time to "kill." The first place he shows up is an unmanned military auxiliary airport, just west of Stockton, to do a touch and go, then onto Hetch Hetchy to honor his promise from the night before. His friend sees Ken's A4 fly into the canyon from west to east at high airspeed, dipping a wing in a hello. Then the aircraft makes a turn to come diving back down the canyon east to west, again at a high speed, then a final pass to the east, entering the canyon slowly, with gear and flaps down, into the high terrain, committing to turning around inside the granite walls. The aircraft disappears around a bend, and the engine sound is dramatic, being magnified by the echo off the cliffs. And as the plane makes its turnaround, the engine speed suddenly accelerates, probably to full power. There were sounds of a crash and an explosion, then silence. The aircraft impacted the canyon walls.

Ken had put himself in an all or nothing situation, obviously done in by his overblown self-confidence! I can only imagine at what point he realized he was done for. By the time this happened the ejection seat option was gone for him; it needs to be a wings-level ejection to work, and he was obviously in a steep turn. Considering that he was below the cliffs, there was no way out!

Addendum: I have an addition to Ken's story that doesn't quite fit in with the above, but thought to include it here because I find it so interesting.

The year before Ken was killed, during our 1967 two weeks training at Fallon, we were part of a scheduled four-plane flight. I was sitting in my aircraft with the engine running, waiting for the rest of the guys, so we could taxi out together, and I'm looking at Ken's plane, which is directly across from me. The engine is running and the ground crew is trying to pull the three landing gear pins, but it is not happening. The pins are jammed. All of the sudden, one of the ground crew runs up the ladder of Ken's plane, reaches inside the cockpit, and pushes the landing gear handle to the "down" position! The aircraft actually jumped off the ground about an inch as

3,000 pounds of hydraulic pressure went to the correct side of the pistons, and all three pin-pullers fell on their backsides.

The story is this: the day before, the plane had been in the hanger with a log book write-up indicating that the guns, etc. could not be fired. There is a safety switch that prevents this if the landing gear is down. This gear switch sometimes needs to be adjusted. The procedure is that the aircraft is on a stand where the operator can raise and lower the gear with a separate hydraulic pump. In this case, the crewmen finally got the switch like they wanted it when the gear was up, then the hydraulic pressure pump was turned off, and the gear extended itself (by gravity) when the pressure bled away. At this point, the pins are put in and the plane is towed back to the outside ramp. But the gear handle is still in the up position! The crewmember who figured out the problem was the guy that left the handle that way!

9
VMA 133: PHIL DELANO

In the spring of 1961 my VMF 133 squadron went through several major changes: first, we moved our base of operations from Oakland Municipal Airport to Naval Air Station Alameda; second, we changed the squadron name from VMF to VMA 133 because we were transiting from a designated fighter aircraft to one whose mission was air to ground attack; and third, we attended a seven-day active duty training period to learn how to fly the new aircraft.

This aircraft was the A4 Skyhawk, a joy to fly and very agile. (The rate of roll was scary - you could fly formation and do an aileron roll to switch from the left wing to the right wing.)

VMA 133 squadron pilots, about thirty of us, showed up on March 23, 1961, for a week of training, and we had a ball! On the last day, April 1, we had finished our final flights and were waiting in the ready room for the last four planes to return. In fact, we had initiated the paperwork to check everyone off of active duty status, so when the last pilots walked in from their flight, we would all be cleared to head for home. It didn't work out that way.

The four-plane division that was still out and just finishing up with tactics decided to do a four-plane in-trail loop to cap off the day. This acrobatic maneuver performed at low altitude in front of a crowd would bring the house down, but at 10,000 feet would be unseen and unappreciated.

The four aircraft arrange themselves nose to tail this way: the lead aircraft is the fixed point that everyone else relates to; the other three aircraft stack themselves behind the leader and each other; the correct and only position that will work is to place the nose of your A4 directly underneath the tail of the aircraft ahead of you, easing the nose up until your rudder pedals start to vibrate from the jet blast coming from the plane ahead. At this point, your plane's nose is about ten feet directly under the tail of the aircraft ahead. Now, all four planes need to hold this position as the flight, during the loop, is going to go from 450 knots at the bottom of the loop to 160 upside down at the top. And if you fall behind, already being at almost full power, you won't be able to catch up!

The four planes descend to build up the airspeed required for the loop. When 450 knots is attained, the lead aircraft starts a smooth 4.5g pull up, putting the division over the top at 160 knots, then heads back down to complete the second half of the maneuver. As the airspeed builds up rapidly, the number three aircraft, flown by Phil Delano, doesn't pull out, and continues straight into the ground! Phil managed to eject, and his parachute was seen drifting down towards Clear Lake, north of Marin County. When paramedics arrived, he was still alive but died shortly thereafter. Evidently, when he ejected, there was a malfunction with his seat - he and the seat separated immediately on ejection, and his body and the aircraft tail collided, which split his pelvic bone in two.

I think the accident board decided that probably when they were at the top of the loop and slow, the horizontal trim for the elevator malfunctioned and moved to the full nose down position. Then, when the airspeed increased during the dive, Phil was not able to overcome the nose down forces and was forced to eject! Probably the high airspeed at the time of ejection caused the immediate seat separation and his collision with the tail.

Phil was a San Francisco firefighter.

10
VMA 133: JOHN B

Three-thirty in the afternoon and the scattered clouds, several thousand feet above me, were reflecting color from the afternoon sun. I remember the rays were angled from slightly below so there was a pink color, almost as though it was setting. Viewing this beauty from 21,000 feet I thought, *this almost makes it worth it.*

The weather had drastically changed from only that morning, when a fast moving front had screamed across the San Francisco Bay Area with high winds, heavy rain, and low clouds. Fortunately, our VMF 133 squadron pilots were not flying, but were in the ready room getting briefed for the morning's flights. All of us, that is, except for two: Del Watts,

TOMMY TINKER

our commanding officer, and John B. were returning from a Southern California air base, and at that time they were approaching the initial fix for an approach back to Alameda. John was in the lead aircraft, and although younger than Del, he had more experience in the A4. Their flight had to be sequenced almost from takeoff to be able to fit into the chaotic situation going on at the major airports in the Bay Area: San Jose and NAS Moffett in the South Bay, plus, just thirty miles northwest, was Oakland and Alameda in the East Bay, and San Francisco on the west side.

The strong pre-frontal winds rolling across the high terrain that surrounds the area, plus thick clouds and driving rain, was making it difficult for Del to stay close enough to maintain his position on John's left side. The A4, with its small wing, is normally easy to fly formation on in an instrument approach; you just keep off to the side, step down and back just enough so you can still see your section leader's hand signals alerting you to impending aircraft configurations, like gear or flaps down. This morning, the task was made much more difficult, partially by the turbulence, which you could kind of roll with because both aircraft were (usually) tossed the same direction as they were so close to each other, but mostly by the reduced visibility due to the heavy rain and very dense clouds, sometimes so thick that Del, having lost visual contact (he was only ten feet away,) was almost forced to break away to the left in fear of a collision.

Bay Approach Control assumed responsibility of the section from Oakland Center during the descent and then passed this control over to Alameda Ground Control Approach (GCA). The flight of A4s was being directed by ground radar to continue descent until breaking out to visual conditions. The first signs of the surface is brown water, angry with 30-knot wind driven waves blowing to the northwest, vague sightings of familiar Bay Area landmarks, and then Alameda's Runway 31 dead ahead. John puts the section in a left turn to get enough spacing from the runway so they can make the right turn back to land in the opposite direction and into the wind.

These two pilots have a lot on their plate! They are about 400 feet above the surface (500 is the legal minimum, but hey, God controls the clouds, and you go as low as you need to when you have only about twenty minutes of fuel left.) The San Francisco-Oakland Bay Bridge is just about two miles north of the runway they are setting up to land on, and the 30-knot tailwind, added to the 150-knot maneuvering speed they need to fly, will make it difficult to stay inside it. (Every twenty seconds they travel a mile.)

Peering through the heavy rain, the "wheels watch" officer at the end of the runway sees the flight starting a right turn to the runway, as the number two aircraft is trying to reduce airspeed to get some separation so they don't land in formation, which is illegal. (What else is new?) This means that Del is trying to slow down, but there isn't much airspeed to play with since John has already had to keep the speed down because the Bay Bridge was so close. One other thing that adds to their problems is that the A4-A aircraft did not have windshield wipers, so as long as they are in a turn and looking out the side, they could see pretty good, but once lined up with the runway, the visibility forward when it's raining is zero! You had to be aware of this and continue using some peripheral vision and a glance at your instruments to keep the wings level, and more or less guess (hope) that the runway is still in front of you.

John, in the number one aircraft, passes the landing end of the runway. The wheels watch officer turns to concentrate on the second aircraft, and is startled to see that he is dangerously close to the water and still descending. Grabbing the radio mike, he starts to shout a warning when he hears the sounds of an aircraft with full power waving off. Turning around, he sees the number one aircraft touching down on the runway *inverted!* The concussion of the crash and the subsequent explosion of the plane overwhelmed any further concerns about Del Watts in the second aircraft.

At 0830 the phone rings in the squadron ready room. Now, this is a tragedy that involves all of us. As a group, we run to a point where we can see the column of black smoke and realize that at least one of our mates has probably perished, but which one? A quick inspection of the aircraft sign out sheets indicates that John was flying the plane that is beneath the pall of flames and smoke on the runway. The skipper, Del, managed to proceed south and get an emergency approach to NAS Moffett, I can only imagine his state of mind as he flew by the burning wreckage, knowing almost certainly that his squadron mate was dead.

John was a San Francisco architect, and our skipper, Del Watts, owned an auto mechanical garage in Sacramento.

11
VMA 133: 6G-28 OR BROKE ON TAKEOFF

Checking out the maintenance write-ups on my assigned aircraft, I noticed that the engine fire warning light had illuminated two flights prior to the one I was scheduled for, and remained on for the duration of that flight. In most military jets, that would usually result in an immediate ejection, but not necessarily in the early A4s. We used to get positive malfunctions fairly regularly.

Taxiing 6G-28, a Douglas built A4-C attack aircraft, onto Runway 25: "cleared for take off, switch to departure control, monitor guard." Brakes on. Signal to Capt. Pete, the wingman ten feet off my left wing tip, to run up the engines to 90% RPM. I visually check his machine - yep, no panels open, horizontal trim is set for take off, canopy locked. My oxygen mask is still hanging loose - no odd smells. I ratchet the right bayonet mask fitting on tight, nod my head, and release the breaks. Ease the throttle forward until my wingman starts to drop back, then retard the throttle a notch so he can hang in there. One hundred-forty knots, back on the stick, gear up, and BAM! Sounds like an explosion! Pete goes by like someone called him to dinner. *A seagull the size of Dumbo must have flown into the engine intake!* This A4 is going down!

We are yawing from side to side. (The tailpipe had separated from the back of the engine and was being slammed around by the exhaust gas. What little thrust came out the back was being vectored left and right.) One hundred feet and descending. Looking out at the end of Runway 25 and San Francisco Bay: *trade airspeed for altitude* - one of the ten commandments for several maneuvers in jet fighters, including ejection at low altitude. At 140 knots, we don't have much to trade, but with the left hand on the ejection curtain, the right pulls back on the stick. Nose up slightly, airspeed now at 130, but at 50 feet above sea level, we're not going down any more. Can't see any boats so I pull the T-handle that allows the two half-full 300-gallon fuel tanks to tumble off the wing, into the bay.

Lighter by 2,000 pounds, the fighter claws itself up to 400 feet. I start a left turn for an approach to Runway 31. Call

Pete telling him I'm on fire and am switching back to tower frequency. He "can't see any smoke." Hard to convince me, staring at a big fire warning light, but the rest of the indications show that we are still at full power. Releasing the ejection curtain, I'm more or less committing to the landing. (The Douglas rocket seat is pretty reliable, having an envelope of operation of no altitude and no airspeed, and we've got a little bit of both, but so many things have to go right, I decide the runway is the "bird in hand" and I'll take it.) I decide to quit struggling for altitude and retard the throttle some to reduce heat back in the coach section. I declare an emergency with the intention of landing on Runway 31, which today has a dangerous crosswind for the A4, but the route back to Runway 25 would be over the city of Alameda, and I would be giving up the option of using the ejection seat with that choice.

"Get out! You're on fire!" was the last radio transmission from Pete, as I touched down and brought the throttle around the horn, shutting off the fuel to the engine. *"Thanks a lot!"* He was now viewing the left side of 6G-28, where yellow flames were joyously peeking out a three by five foot hole. So far, so good. *Keep it straight.* Full left rudder and enough brake to keep her from drifting down wind. I can't use the right break to help slow down because with the strong crosswind it, will take us off the runway. *Can't breathe.* The O2 mask is suffocating me (oxygen bottle had exploded). Mask off. As 6G-28 slowed down, the rudder became less effective, so

I had to use more left breaking to keep on the center line. *Come on baby. Don't drift on me.* Aiming for the center of the arresting gear, hook down, still 90 knots. If we miss the gear, we're going in the Bay.

Didn't miss! Caught the cable dead center. Canopy open, surrounded by white smoke, outta here! *Don't break a leg. Got a long way to go.* Walked on air for about seventy-five yards and stopped to watch her burn. *Wonder how far that jet fuel will go when she blows up.* Ran some more. Did that about three times till 6G-28 was about two football fields away.

When I saw her at the hanger a few hours later, I had a feeling like we had kinda saved each other. She hung together long enough for me to get us back on the ground, and I didn't give up on her and take my chances with the ejection seat.

12
VMA 133: TONY - MCAS EL TORO

The A4-C Skyhawk and its sister models had a safety feature with the throttle system so that if there was a mechanical disconnection from the throttle in the pilot's hand to the fuel control unit on the engine, the engine power would stabilize at 87 percent. This ensured enough thrust to allow the aircraft to at least maintain level flight. Supposedly, when the pilot wanted to slow the plane down and descend to land, he would increase drag by opening the speed breaks, lowering the landing gear, and then controlling the angle of descent to the runway by varying the amount of flaps, slowing enough (about 140 knots) that the slats on the leading edge of the wing extended. Once on the ground, since he had no direct control over the engine speed, it would be necessary to cut off fuel to the engine. In a normal situation, this was done by moving the throttle to idle, then around the horn to the "fuel off" position. In an abnormal situation like this, the only way to shut down the engine was by moving another handle, the fuel control lever, to the "off" position. These two methods for shutting down the engine differed in that, bringing the throttle around the horn cut the fuel off at the fuel control unit, and the engine shut down immediately, while, when using the fuel control lever, the fuel was cut off at the fuel tank and the engine would continue to run until the fuel line from the tank to the fuel control unit was empty. This could take a fatally long time! At least two of my friends have been killed this way.

Tony, whose civilian job was flying with Pan American Airlines, was on a night cross country with Marine Corps Air Station El Toro, California, as his destination. Some time during the flight, the engine stopped responding to the throttle movements and the engine power stabilized at 87 percent. Los Angeles Center, Orange County Approach Control, and later MCAS El Toro tower personnel, were informed of the situation and told that, after touchdown, he intended to drop the hook (designed for carrier landings), and catch the arresting gear at the far end of the runway.

The approach and landing were successful, but during roll out, the engine thrust reduced to idle without any further commands from the cockpit. For some reason, Tony must have decide that he once again had control of the engine speed and told the crash crew and tower that he would taxi to the ramp on his own. Unfortunately, this was not to be. When the plane turned off the runway on to a taxiway, the engine speed suddenly increased back up to 87 percent. The brakes on the A4 are capable of keeping a fully loaded plane with a total weight of about 24,000 pounds from moving, even at 100 per-cent of power, but at landing weights of around 10,000 pounds, Tony's plane started to rapidly increase speed, even though the breaks were full on. He brought the throttle around the horn, and when the engine stayed at high power, moved the fuel control lever to the "off" position. The aircraft speed still increased, waiting for the fuel to be exhausted. The left tire blew and the metal wheel started to grind down. The right tire blew and two red streaks of burning metal were tracking the plane's path towards a large fuel truck. Just before colliding with the truck, Tony pulled the ejection curtain.

The A4-C is equipped with a Douglas rocket seat for ejection. Most pilots that ride on it appreciate the fact that, being powered by a rocket, the acceleration is a bit more gentle than the Martin Baker seat used in other Navy planes, which use an explosive charge to catapult the pilot free of his craft (most pilots that have used it sustain damage to their spine). Fighter pilots ride on a very hard chair because both of these ejection systems are capable of breaking the thigh bones if a cushion allows the seat to start accelerating before the pilot does.

This seat is designed to save a pilot's life, even if he ejects with no altitude and no airspeed, but lots of things must happen perfectly. First, the canopy is blown off, and the seat is propelled up the tracks, causing the pilot's feet to swing back by centrifugal force to just miss the windscreen. A small explosion disconnects the seat belt then a balloon inflates to separate the body from the seat. A small "pilot" chute is deployed to help pull out the parachute then the skirt of the main chute is opened by another propellant. To allow time for all this to happen, a height of about 200 feet is required (no wonder there are some back injuries.)

In Tony's case, none of this happened. He was shot up over a hanger to die, still strapped in the seat. Just the breaks of Marine Air.

TOMMY TINKER

In 1951, this Edna, TX high school graduate hoped for a career in the ocean as a commercial diver.

Navy flight school. The T-6 Texan was the first plane I ever flew. Then Major John Glenn was my first instructor!

With my friend and fellow cadet, Russell French (left).

My first jet aircraft, the TV-2.

Flying the T-28.

Not my regulation flight suit. Pensacola was hot!

Aboard the USS Monterey. Cadets had to complete six carrier landings.

With fellow cadets in winter and summer uniforms. (I am 2nd from left.)

My mother, Flossie, pinned wings onto my uniform after graduation from Navy flight school.

Marine Corps Second Lt. Tommy Tinker.

First airplane rides for my maternal grandmother and little niece, in Charlie, the first of five airplanes I owned.

VMF 232, MCAS Kaneohe Bay, Hawaii. The sleek FJ-2 would go through the speed of sound in a dive!

TOMMY TINKER

THE "FLYING FINS" skin diving club receives instructions from club president Tom Tinker as he points out the various uses of the living lung on Pete Parmenter. Attentive pupils front row (l to r) Dave Lougee, Ted Lingenfelter, Walt Telford, Bob Martin, and Bob Smith. Back row "Doc" Kellner, Bill Osborne, and Lock Bridenstine.

At the Marine base in Japan, the Flying Fins were so named because the water around the base was lousy for diving. The military would fly us to Okinawa for a week where the diving was gorgeous! I remember watching a small snake dive to almost 100' and go back to the surface for a small breath, then dive again.

Me and my Plymouth, which I had shipped to Japan.

Life at the Marine base in Japan.

The AD-5 with radar pod on its belly.

The gorgeous F-86 fought the MiG 17 in Korea.

13
FUNNY, DUMB STUNTS

Ornithopter

It's really not my fault; it's just that whenever there was an opportunity to pull some funny (dumb) stunt, regardless of the ramifications, I usually couldn't stop myself. Like the time the new commanding officer of our reserve squadron was giving us a spit and polish lecture about what a poor excuse for Marines we had become and I released an ornithopter (one of those artificial flying birds made of paper and wire, powered by a rubber band) from the back of the room, at the same time shouting, "Oh my God!" It flew low over the seated pilots straight to the Colonel who started swatting at it with his swagger stick. It whapped him right on the nose and fell to the floor, where he stomped on it and threw it out the window, and - can you believe it - never said a word. I knew that it could have been the end of my military career but I couldn't help it. The joke was too good, the opportunity too great!

Tarantula

It was a long taxi from the terminal to the takeoff end of the runway in Stockton, California, which gave me ample opportunity to switch the jar with the tarantula in it from Captain Dan's open nav bag - which sat between us on the step to the cockpit of the Martin 404 - to my bag, out of sight on my right, with the empty jar I had brought along for the purpose. The tarantula was a gift from me to Danny, to give to his son for a high school biology class.

By the time we got the "cleared for takeoff," things were set up like I wanted them: the empty jar, with the lid off and lying there, next to the jar with the bat. Oh yes, we had acquired a bat during the hour-long layover. The Stockton tower folks had invited us up, and while there, one of them brought in a bat, which we promptly took charge of. Danny's son's biology class was going to be very lively. (The kid later got bit by a rattlesnake he had in a jar!)

As the Danny steered the plane onto the runway, he took his hand off the throttles and said, "Ok Tom, you got it." As he did this, his eye caught the open jar, and he started making strange, unintelligible sounds, like "aahhu-aahhu," as he attempted to steer the plane back onto the taxiway.

Several things went through my mind, like delays, explanations to the chief pilot, etc. So, moving the throttles forward, I forced the takeoff. "We gotta go Danny! There's a plane on short final." (A lie.) After we got the gear up and throttled back to climb power, I said, "Dan, what's the problem?" He blurts, "The bat's out! The bat's out!" After leaving the tower frequency (and cancelling our IFR clearance), it was decided that I would see if I could find "the bat."

Standing in the cargo compartment and looking forward, I felt compassion. Danny was flying the airplane almost without touching it. The points of contact were minimal: very little with the seat (covering as small a space as he had since he was maybe eight years old, made possible by a pair of very tense muscles), only the balls of his feet touched the rudders, and just two fingers of each hand were handling the yoke. His blue shirt was soaked and the hair on the back of his neck was standing up. It didn't help much when I said, "Danny, it's not the bat. It's the tarantula that's out!"

Now, I definitely didn't know what to do next, so decided to take one step at a time. After a moment or so, I told him that I had found and killed it. It took about five minutes for Danny's breathing to start to return to normal. As soon as we got to the gate and the engines were shut down in SFO, I produced the jar with the live tarantula. It took about thirty seconds for him to figure it out. At first he thought it was funny, but the rest of the month's conversation was mostly limited to "gear up" and "gear down." I don't think I got to even fly a leg.

You gotta know, I didn't plan for it to happen on takeoff. I figured he would discover the open jar en-route, we would have a laugh (after the initial reaction), I'd tease him a little about scaring the flight attendant with the thing in Stockton, which he had done. (She was so shook up that she got off the flight in SFO.) It would be our little joke and we would still be friends. Kinda worked that way, but it took a bit longer than I had hoped.

14
LIFE AFTER DEATH

I am not a religious person, although I wish I were. I would like to believe in a life beyond the one we are now living and have tried to be open to that possibility, but, except for two situations, I have seen little to convince me that some part of our being carries on. The two instances do provide food for thought.

One morning, about a week after my mother-in-law died, my then wife, Matilda, told me that the previous night her mother had appeared, standing by the bed, and called her name then just smiled at her and disappeared. Matilda told me what her mom was wearing and was adamant that she was not asleep! She had been suffering with great sadness and I feel that her mom had appeared to comfort her.

The only other occasion that allowed me to peek through a crack in the spirit world wall happened at work. In May of 1964, I was preparing for an early morning flight with Pacific Airlines. The captain and I would be flying a 28-passenger DC-3 from San Francisco, south through several coastal cities to Los Angeles. With the paperwork completed, we still had a little time to kill, so we decided to have one more cup of coffee before heading out. Just as the skipper started down the stairs to the coffee shop, I was knocked to my knees by a black wave of energy. If I hadn't grabbed the stair railing, I think I would have been driven to the floor. I don't remember any sound, but I was overwhelmed by sadness and despair. Then it was over, gone as fast as it had arrived.

For some reason, I looked up at the clock on the wall: 6:33 AM. We later found out that was the moment Pacific Airlines Flight 773, with forty-three souls onboard, was deliberately crashed into the ground by a crazed gunman after he shot the crew to death!

Was I the only person who experienced that black wave of sadness and despair? Was a friend or loved one onboard that made me the first recipient of the bad news? All I have found out is that I only knew the three crewmembers, and I wasn't close to any of them. I must have just been in the way!

15
CHALLENGER DISASTER

On the morning of the Space Shuttle "Challenger" loss, I was flying from Miami to Detroit. It was a beautiful, clear, *cold,* day. Our route took us along the western coastline of the Florida peninsula, where we had a bright, clear view of the Kennedy Space Center, with Challenger sitting on the launch pad and pre-launch steam billowing from the base of the rocket. We knew the launch was being delayed because of the cold and were disappointed that we were not going to have the front row seat for launch we thought we might.

As we approached the Tallahassee area, we heard a transmission that sounded like, "They have launched Challenger!" Another voice chimed in, "Great! They have launched Challenger!" "No, they lost it! It exploded!" No other transmissions.

    I decided not to speak of it to the passengers. They would find out soon enough, but I became aware, mostly by the stunned silence of my fellow comrades, maybe six or seven aircrew in radio range for this conversation, how we, all of us Americans, share a common connection through our nation's triumphs and failures.

16
SMX CRASH

In 1959, Pacific Airlines had a contract to operate daily round-trip flights from Los Angeles to Catalina Island. The single DC-3 aircraft was based in LAX and didn't cycle through the San Francisco maintenance base, so daily mechanical upkeep was performed by a locally contracted firm.

In October of that year, the flight crews became concerned about the left engine when they started noticing an oil leak on the ramp every morning as they came out to start the day. After much reluctance, the company agreed to bring the craft up to SFO to be repaired. Unfortunately, they elected to fly it up as a "revenue flight," with paying passengers onboard. The flight stopped at Oxnard and then Santa Maria

(SMX). While at the gate in Santa Maria, one of the agents called the crew's attention to oil dripping (pouring) from the left engine's cowling, and after checking it out, the cockpit crew decided to continue the flight.

A personal observation here: The co-pilot was Joe Flannigan, who was in the process of checking out as captain. The check captain was a very difficult individual to fly with and offered no help in decision-making. I personally feel that Joe was intimidated into continuing the flight, even after he expressed concern about the oil leak and the continuing capabilities of that engine to function.

Upon takeoff from SMX, the left engine exploded, sending the #5 cylinder through the cowling, which was deformed to the extent that the resulting drag prevented the aircraft from being able to maintain flight. It crashed one and a half miles north of the airport! Every one of the seventeen passengers and the flight attendant survived, as did the check captain, although he was severely injured. Unfortunately, Flannigan ended up underneath the plane and was crushed when the front of the plane impacted a heavy steel cattle gate.

17

MEDFORD TO CRESCENT CITY, 1960: ADVANCES IN TECHNOLOGY

It is almost impossible to describe the effect that the jet transport and Very High Frequency (VHF) radio aids, mated with distance measuring equipment, have made in aviation, but I'll relate some true situations that may help explain their impact. In the era of piston engines, with low-altitude icing, non-heated windshields, etc., pilots had to use as much concentration to keep the airplane flying as they did navigating.

On an instrument approach in icing conditions, the non-flying pilot was almost totally involved in keeping hot air flowing through the carburetors. Every time the throttles were moved, the carburetor heat controls had to be readjusted.

Flying a Martin 404 one dark night over southern California (with a piston-powered engine and a zillion moving parts, like a car,) my good friend, Capt. Mac, said, "Tom, give me some carburetor heat. I think we've got ice." (Fuel flow was rising. If fuel flow is increasing, the ice in the carburetor is in the "A" chamber and if it is decreasing it is in the "B" chamber. Each case requires opposite procedures.) As I reached for the levers, Mac said, "One at a time, please," as he instinctively moved both fuel mixtures to full rich. (Wrong!) Both engines quit and almost auto-feathered before he got the mixtures back where they had been. "Yeah, Mac, one at a time." (The passengers didn't have to use the bathroom for the rest of that flight.)

As to the jet engines: I experienced three engine shutdowns, caused by fire or failure, in my first 2,000 hours with the airlines. All were piston-powered engines. And I experienced *zero* shutdowns the last 25,000 hours with jet engines.

Non-heated windshields? Well, sometimes there was so much ice on the DC-3 that we had to open a small window on either side of the windshield to see the runway. If there was a crosswind, the pilot that could see the runway best made the landing. In contrast, I have never seen solid ice on a jet's windshield because they are electrically heated.

VHF navigation aids give uninterrupted, strong, accurate signals to guide the aircraft. But on many of our routes in the early 60s, we still navigated with Low Frequency (LF) beacons, and even some commercial broadcast stations. They could be received at a longer distance than VHF, but the signal was neither strong nor accurate.

Flying from Medford, Oregon to Crescent City, California with Capt. Jack, we were faced with strong headwinds from the west, lots of icing at 8,000 feet, and turbulence *(to stay at altitude: gear down and idle power on the updrafts, and keep a clean airplane with full power on the down drafts.)* At our predetermined time to cross the Crescent City beacon, we saw the Automatic Direction Finder (ADF) needle switch from pointing forward to pointing behind us, indicating station passage. I called this out to Capt. Jack since we had 8,000 feet to loose, and he hadn't started down yet. (We were supposedly over the Pacific Ocean by now.) "Yeah, hold on a bit," he told me. About forty seconds later, the needle turned to point ahead of us again, held steady about two minutes, then swung back to point behind us. We were both spooked by this time, so we maintained our altitude. Sure enough, the needle turned back to the nose, then switched back to the tail about three minutes later. Capt. Jack then started his descent and we landed in about seventeen minutes. Turns out that the LF antenna on the ground at Crescent City was being blown onto a tin roof and shorting out, at which time the ADF needle would turn and point to the closest thunderstorm, which was behind us. Experience, caution, and fear saved us back then!

One advantage that LF had over VHF was that you could dial in a commercial broadcast station and design your own approach to an emergency field, in case you couldn't maintain altitude because of icing or engine failure.

18
CHICO TO MARYSVILLE, 1960

Heading south, trying to follow the right highway, *that row of lights must go to Beal Air Force Base; the ones that turn slightly more westward go to Marysville. I think. Oh yeah, I see the drive-in theater. Where's the green and white rotating light for the airport? Was that it? There it is again. Got to wait for the green one to be sure. OK!*

I had been in a 500 feet per minute (fpm) rate of descent for three minutes (since the DC-3 was un-pressurized, that was the maximum rate we could use to prevent passengers having problems with their ears,) and now, at 1,500', I was looking for the runway lights. *Why do they make 'um so directional? Can't see the buggers unless we're almost lined* up. *That rotating beacon doesn't give me any idea how far away I am...guess I'll keep going down.*

Captain Mel will start to squirm when I get below 1,000' if I'm not pretty close to a three-degree slope to the touch down spot. Slight right turn to find the runway lights. Yeah, there they are. Gear down, flaps one quarter, slight left turn to line up. *Think I'm about right on the altitude but what's a 4,500' runway supposed to look like if I'm on altitude?* Chico's runway was 6,000' long and 200' wide. Would a 4,500' runway that is 150' wide give the same illusion?

Captain Mel doesn't look like he's squirming so I keep on trucking. Got my full flaps, over the threshold. *Sure is black out there. Yeah, this is what a 150' wide runway looked like when I pulled the throttles to idle last time, so lets do it. Felt a little ground cushion there - nose up a little more.* Squeak. Squeak. Slight forward pressure on the yoke. Ease the tail down, breaking just enough to make the turn off. Unlock the tail wheel and get off the runway to let Captain Mel take us to the gate.

Man, I'm feeling pretty smug. Only got myself about 800 hours total, and maybe 50 in the DC-3, and already getting so I can squeak 'um on. I notice Mel has brought the plane to a halt and we aren't to the gate yet. He's just staring at me with his mouth open.

"Sir?"

"Jesus Christ! Why didn't you turn on the landing lights?"

Now, my momma may have raised a fool, but not a dumb fool, so I blurted, "What?! This aircraft has landing lights? I've never flown a plane that had landing lights!"

Mel's jaw dropped even further, then he shook his head and never mentioned it again.

Even though I had just forgotten to turn on the DC-3's lights and was trying to alibi myself, what I said was the truth. None of the planes I flew in the military had landing lights. We just noted how far apart the runway lights were during the takeoff roll, then when we came back to land, assumed our landing attitude when the lights looked the same. Of course, the Navy wanted you to fly the jets onto the runway without flaring, so I guess lights wouldn't make much difference - just scare the hell out of you.

19
NIGHT FLIGHT

Entering a right downwind traffic pattern for Runway 13 at the Chico Municipal Airport, we see an aircraft beacon flashing below us in the approach area for the runway we intend to land on. Chico is an "uncontrolled" airport, meaning that aircraft transiting the area make their intentions known by broadcasting "in the blind" on a standard radio frequency to everyone in the area. Anyone who hears that transmission is required to respond in kind. We make the call and declare our intentions. Not getting a response, we assume that the aircraft we are watching is just passing through the area and not monitoring the local radio frequency. Captain Bob, who is flying the airplane, makes a right turn to base leg and is descending to traffic pattern altitude. It is at this point that the no-radio light plane starts to become a problem. Even though he seems to be just passing through and not landing, his position and altitude are inhibiting our ability to get to the approach end of the runway.

Our DC9-30 is capable of flying a high rate of descent, which Capt. Bob now initiates: throttles at idle, spoilers (speed brakes) fully extended, and max traffic pattern airspeed. It is extremely dark outside; except for the beacon on the light plane and the one beacon at the airport it's like flying in an inkwell. There are no farm or road lights, no stars, etc., to give us some depth perception, and no horizon!

I look at Bob, his full concentration is on the light plane and I realize that with no horizon and surface lights we won't be able to tell when we are below his altitude. I survey the situation again and am startled by our precarious position! I wait a moment longer then say "Bob, we're only 1,500 feet above the ground and we're descending at 2,500 feet per minute!" (In 45 seconds we will be dead!) His reaction was to calmly add power, bring the spoilers in, and establish the aircraft in a level flight attitude then continue to the airport and make a normal approach and landing.

As we were deplaning our passengers, Bob turned to me and said, "Tommy, what did you say to me out there on our approach?" I repeated my comment and he said, "You know, I didn't have a clue." Even so, Bob was one of the most professional pilots I have ever flown with!

20
PILOT PUSHING

In the early days, the airline company's concept of how to make a profit was to have the shortest times possible between destinations, and with good reason, as crewmember salaries and fuel costs were directly tied to the length of time we were airborne. Pacific Airlines approached the problem of making its pilots more efficient by rewarding those who had the fastest times between stops by giving them their first choice of the next month's lines of time (flights arranged in a sequence of days to give the most days off while flying close to the maximum pay time for the month.)

Captain Knox Pittman was usually the winner every month. Somehow, he was able to consistently fly the fastest times between our destination cities. I say "somehow" but it wasn't a mystery; while other pilots were flying long, involved instrument approaches, Knox would bypass the approach and fly through the clouds to where he thought the airport was. One Captain that I flew with said he was with Knox when he descended into the fog trying for the Santa Maria airport. As they gradually began to see the ground, they realized they were surrounded by mountain peaks! Knox asked for climb power while commenting that he wasn't where he thought he was!

The DC-3 did not have pressurization, so the crews were restricted to a maximum descent rate of 500 feet per minute, which was to minimize discomfort for the passengers' ears. This requirement just meant the pilots had to do a little more planning on their approach and landing so they didn't have to make a circle over their destination airport while they were "getting the passengers ears down." There was one route that usually required at least one circle and that was coming from the north to land at Santa Barbara, California. A 5,000 foot ridge kept us up so that, once we could start down, we were too close to the airport to go straight in - hence, the one circle.

For everybody except Knox Pittman, that is. Knox would cross the ridge almost 500 feet lower than anyone else, even at night! His theory was that if you could see the lights of the city, there wasn't a mountain between you and your destination. And he was right in a way. The night he hit the mountain with upwards of twenty passengers on board, the cockpit of the DC-3 got over to the Santa Barbara side but the rest of the aircraft did not.

21
BLOSSOM FLIGHTS

Pacific Airlines was a funky little airline that only had a couple of destinations outside of California, like Medford and Eugene, Oregon, but they had some unique operations, which I found intriguing.

In the early 1960s, the South San Francisco Bay Area (west San Jose) was heavily planted with fruit trees. Every spring, the area was awash in blooms, so Pacific Airlines ran a series of "Blossom Flights." They would load up twenty-eight folks in a DC-3 and do a forty-five-minute or so scenic tour of the South Bay, with the seatbelt sign off and cockpit door open. The passengers could move about the cabin for the best viewing.

Fast-forward to today and you will see that where the orchards used to be are now solid homes. And if you look closely, you will notice that in almost every back yard is one fruit tree, which every season bears more than one family could possibly eat!

Pacific also had scheduled flights between Van Nuys in Southern California and Catalina Island, using the DC-3. We had about six crewmembers who had their own mini domicile in Van Nuys and served the island once or twice a day. The biggest worry there was that the crews did not hit a buffalo on the Catalina runway, as the animals roamed freely there.

22
FORMATION APPROACH TO SFO

We have been cleared for a visual approach to San Francisco's Runway 1 behind a TWA 707, which is about three miles ahead of us. The procedure only requires that we follow TWA to the airport and land behind him with safe separation. Both aircraft are to visually fly a path that keeps us over the Bay to the initial approach position for Runway 28, then make a left turn to position us for the ninety degree base leg to Runway 1. The track we are flying will put us over the heavily populated townships on the peninsula, just to the west of the Bayshore Freeway, a seldom used approach to SFO Airport, only required when the winds blow strongly from the north.

It is a gorgeous, clear, dark night in the Bay Area. We

are slightly higher than TWA so their lights are blending into those on the ground; only the red flashing beacon is a visible identity of their aircraft. We see them cross over the outer marker for Runway 28 then start a left turn, which will position them for the right base leg to Runway 1. We are flying a twin engine, high wing, slow moving, 40-passenger F-27, so Captain George flies us well past the point where the TWA 707 made their left turn before we make ours. We start into the landing checklist with gear down, flaps approach setting, passengers seated, etc. We're both involved with required tasks other than just flying as we position ourselves for the final landing phase of the flight. Heads up now, my vision, both peripheral and focused, takes in our part of the Bay Area, and I see that something is missing. TWA!

"Hey, George, where is that TWA we're supposed to be following?" He goes, "Shit!" adds power and starts to level off. (We had been rapidly descending.) About that instant, the TWA fly's directly beneath us! We are so directly on top of him I can see lights from the passenger windows on both sides of the 707. Being that they were only about 30 knots faster than us, it took more than just an instant for them to get gone! It was like being in a subway station and watching a bypass train go through. We even had time to hope that the tail didn't clip us as it passed under. It was that close!

We would have been almost totally at fault because our instructions were to "follow TWA" but I can't imagine that he didn't see our beacon in front of him. Of course, he wasn't expecting us, was he?

23
YOU *CAN* TEACH AN OLD DOG NEW TRICKS

When Northwest retired the Boeing 727, the staff at Retired Northwest Pilot's Association (RNPA) asked for 727 stories. I didn't think I had anything to offer because I only flew it for a year as a First Officer, but have now decided that it might be interesting to write about the introduction of the aircraft to Pacific Airlines. Pacific got three 727-100s in 1966. None of the initial Captains had ever flown pure jet equipment but, boy, did they learn fast!

Our most challenging route was a twelve-landing day that started in SFO and went to LAX with stops in Monterey (MRY) and Santa Barbara (SBA). We made two complete round trips a day. At the time, there was no speed restriction below 10,000 feet, so we would accelerate to 340 knots as soon as we got out of the airport restricted area. The only place we ever leveled off was between Monterey and Santa Barbara, where we got a five-minute cruise break. When we started down, we were already at VMO (maximum airspeed at which the aircraft is certified to operate) of 390 knots, and we kept that speed until we approached the airport or initial approach fix.

We had no altitude reminders (pilots made their own) and no proximity warning. The MRY Runway 28 had a one and a half degree down slope, and was just over 4,500 feet long with a 200-foot drop at the end. But we soon learned that the 727 was much more aerodynamically precise than the Fairchild F-27 we had been flying. Circling approaches were a piece of cake (we could do that then,) plus, when you wanted to stop, you had great braking, even from the nose wheel. Reverse thrust was variable so you could pull in as much as you needed (the F-27 props just went to flat pitch, and even terror wouldn't increase their effect.)

We were always pretty light, even with a full passenger load, because we didn't have much fuel on board, so the landing speeds were sloooow. We flew the approach at 115 knots and touched down at 110. (The DC-9 and -10, with no wing leading-edge devices, had landing speeds up to 133 knots.) When we landed on the down slope runway at MRY, more times than not, we would turn off at the center intersection, after just about 2,000 feet, without abusing the brakes. (Honest.) Finally, the tower folks told us we had to go to go to the next intersection before turning off. We did that until one day, we stuck the static wicks on the right wing tip through the rudder of a light twin that was parked near that turn-off.

SBA had a 5,000-foot runway, and further north, Arcata, which was reputed to be the foggiest airport in the U.S., had 5,900 feet with a 200-foot drop off on both ends. Plus, with weather, there was always a 10-knot tailwind on Arcata's runway. My first landing with braking action 'nil' was at Yakima, WA, with less than 7,000 feet of runway. (You could do that then also.)

The only incident that I can remember in the several years of this operation was caused by the fact that Boeing's checklist kept the anti-skid switch on after landing, and a stray signal released the brakes one morning just as one of our planes was pulling up to the jetway in SFO (ask Jimmy Douglas and Pete Peterson.) Moving at about five knots, that little airplane destroyed the jetway, plus that part of the terminal and was back flying in about three months. The aircraft, not the jetway.

24
INTERESTING DAY DAY AT THE OFFICE

The DC-10 that we are flying is a tight fit for the Honolulu-Sydney (HNL-SYD) route, meaning that when we lift off the HNL runway and head south, we are usually at maximum weight of 600,000 pounds: full passenger load of 290 and full fuel tanks, enough to get us to our destination, but no further. On this particular trip, we end up in a holding pattern at 0645 in the morning because Sydney won't allow approaches over the city until 0700 (don't want to wake those Aussies up too early), and we are almost out of fuel. With only 17,000 pounds in our tanks, having used over 215,000 pounds during the ten-hour trip south, our engines will quit in about forty minutes, and the closest alternate, either Cairns or Melbourne, is over an hour away.

I am chatting with the check Captain (yes, the last check ride of my career--that may sound ominous!) about our predicament, low fuel, no alternate airport, etc., and he acknowledged, then mentioned that he didn't think it was a big deal because the weather report indicated we should break out of the clouds at 1,500 feet, which was what I expected given the current weather report.

Finally, we're given a vector heading to intercept the localizer and then "cleared for the approach." We stay at 3,000 feet until the glide slope indicator starts to guide us down to the runway. Even though the prescribed procedure was to let the autopilot fly the approach, I decide to turn it off and "hand fly" the airplane. This is a mistake because the weather had a surprise for us. The normal procedure was to use the autopilot to fly the plane because it is much more precise then we humans, and being low on fuel, we *have* to land, but the weather report indicated that there was a high ceiling at the airport and I went with it.

We enter the cloud tops at about 2,500 feet and descend into darkness. The lower we go, the worse the weather is. At 1,500 feet, where we are supposed to break out of the clouds, the rain is so loud we have a hard time communicating with each other. At this point I'm wondering if I can get the autopilot hooked back up. Through 1,000 feet, then 700, and things are not getting any better. At 500 feet and still in thick rain and clouds, I decide that we could not miss this approach. We don't have enough fuel to try again, and even if we did, there was nowhere else to go, so we're committed to continue down until the wheels touch the ground, whether I can see it or not! At 300 feet we break out of the clouds to a very windy and wet runway. We land with about an inch and a half of water on the ground, and with a slight tailwind, so we use all the runway on our landing roll then taxied to the terminal, shutting down with just a little over 10,000 pounds of fuel. We left Hawaii with 230,000 pounds!

    I flew the HNL-SYD trip about twenty-seven times and that is the only one that requires that we fly an instrument.

EPILOGUE

Corpus Christi to Cuba in a Sailboat

Ahh retirement. It was easy to imagine, while trying to sleep in one of the very small bunks on either side of the engine, which my younger brother, Douglas, called the "afterberths," that maybe I had been swallowed by a large mammal and was somewhere in it's digestive system. The sounds of sloshing, squirting, gurgling and rumbling, plus fluids (digestive?) that drip, rather continuously, on your body when this boat is underway at sea, add to that impression, and make you wonder if you are not further along in the digestive process than you want to be!

www.ingramcontent.com/pod-product-compliance
Lightning Source LLC
Chambersburg PA
CBHW051954290426
44110CB00015B/2241